CRAFT

IDEAS FOR 4s AND 5s

x

Craft Ideas for 4s and 5s I
DAVID C. COOK PUBLISHING CO.
Elgin, Illinois/Weston, Ontario
CRAFT IDEAS FOR 4s AND 5s I
© 1991 David C. Cook Publishing Co.

Published by David C. Cook Publishing Co.
850 North Grove Avenue, Elgin, IL 60120
Cable Address: DCCOOK
ISBN: 1-55513-413-0

Project Editors
Debbie Paschang
Nancy Raney

Editors
Robin Currie
Dave and Neta Jackson
Ramona Warren

Designers
Dawn Lauck
Donna Kae Nelson

Illustrator
Barbara Todd

Contributing Writers
Carl Heine
Neta Jackson
Lois Keffer
Brenda and Donald Ratcliff
Anna Trimiew
Ramona Warren

Little hands love to be busy! Fat crayons, glue sticks, and construction paper in lots of colors invite children to become creative. With a little planning these objects can do more than just keep preschoolers busy!

Making crafts can help young children feel good about things they create and help them learn to use their hands in new ways. Crafts can also remind preschoolers of what they've learned about God and what He has done. That's what the crafts in this book are designed to do!

Each of these 53 crafts reinforces a theme about God that is appropriate for 4s and 5s. Use these ideas whenever you want to teach young children about God—in children's church, Sunday school, midweek club, day care—even at home. Some crafts include patterns which you may photocopy. All require only readily available, inexpensive supplies.

Let *Craft Ideas for 4s and 5s I* help you remind preschoolers of special things about God. You'll enjoy leading 4s and 5s to praise God through the works of their hands!

THANK YOU, GOD NAPKIN RINGS

For each napkin ring, children will need a copy of the "Thank You, God" strip on this page and a 1 1/2" section of paper towel or toilet paper tube. (Encourage children to make a napkin ring for each member of their families.) Children can color the strips and cut them out. Glue each strip around a section of tube to form a napkin ring. Then cover each ring with clear, self-adhesive paper to make it more durable.

THINGS YOU'LL NEED:

- ❑ Copies of the "Thank You, God" strip for each child
- ❑ Paper towel or toilet paper tubes
- ❑ Scissors
- ❑ Glue
- ❑ Crayons
- ❑ Clear plastic adhesive paper (optional)

2 **HELPER POCKET**

THINGS YOU'LL NEED:

☐ Copies of the "Helper Pocket" pattern for each child
☐ Pocket backs (cut from construction paper)
☐ Construction paper
☐ Scissors
☐ Markers or crayons
☐ Glue or stapler
☐ Band-Aids
☐ Safety pins

Give each child a copy of the "Helper Pocket" pattern and a pocket back. Have the children color the words "Helper Pocket." They might also decorate the pockets with stickers and other art materials before cutting them out.

Help the children glue or staple the front and back of their pockets together. If using glue, run a thin line along the edge of one of the pockets.

Give each child a Band-Aid to slip inside of the pocket. Also, attach a small safety pin to the top edge of the pocket. Help the children pin the pockets on their clothing. Tell them they can put things in their pockets that can help others.

STAND-UP FIGURE

Each child will need a copy of the "Stand-up Figure," a cardboard figure for backing, and a 1" x 6" strip of cardboard. The children can color the paper figures to resemble a parent (mom or dad) who helps them. Assist them as needed in cutting out the figures and along the dotted lines of the heart so it opens like a door. Glue the paper figure to the cardboard one, matching edges. Inside the heart opening, write "Thank You, God" for each child. Fold the cardboard strip in half and glue one side to the back of the cardboard figure. The figure will stand. The children can place the "Stand-up Figure" where they will remember to thank God for parents who help them.

THINGS YOU'LL NEED:

- ❑ Copies of the "Stand-up Figure" for each child
- ❑ Lightweight cardboard figures for backing
- ❑ Strips of cardboard 1" x 6"
- ❑ Scissors
- ❑ Crayons
- ❑ Glue
- ❑ Fine-point marking pen

My Parents Help Me

4 I LOVE YOU PAPERWEIGHT

THINGS YOU'LL NEED:

❑ Smooth rocks, blocks of wood, or lumps of hardened clay
❑ Markers
❑ Paints
❑ Polyurethane or other varnish (optional)

Give each child a smooth rock, lump of hardened clay, or block of wood. Let the children paint and decorate the paperweights. Help them print the words, "I Love You," on the paperweights with markers, and also print their names on them. You might help the children draw decorations of hearts, stars, or flowers. If possible, cover the paperweights with a coat of polyurethane or other varnish.

FRIENDSHIP TREE

Give a copy of the "Friendship Tree" to each child. Children can color the tree trunk, grass, and sky. Then show children how to crumple scraps of tissue paper in various fall colors (red, yellow, orange, and green tissue) and glue them to the branches of the tree as leaves.

Have the children tell you the names of friends to print around the leaves.

THINGS YOU'LL NEED:

- ❑ Copies of the "Friendship Tree" for each child
- ❑ Red, yellow, orange, green tissue paper
- ❑ Fine-point marking pens
- ❑ Glue
- ❑ Crayons

My Friendship tree

6 MY BEST FRIEND

THINGS YOU'LL NEED:

- ❑ Copies of "My Best Friend" picture for each child
- ❑ Construction paper
- ❑ Scissors
- ❑ Glue
- ❑ Glitter (optional)
- ❑ Hole punch
- ❑ Yarn or ribbon

Give each child a copy of the "My Best Friend" picture, a sheet of construction paper, and a 9" x 12" length of yarn or ribbon. Children can color the pictures then glue them to the sheets of construction paper. If you wish, decorate the construction paper frames with glue and glitter. As a final step, punch two holes at the top of each picture and help children tie yarn or ribbon hangers.

My Best Friend

JESUS LOVES YOU PUZZLE

7

Give each child a copy of the puzzle page to color. For added durability, glue the colored picture to light cardboard and cover with a clear, self-adhesive paper. Help the children cut the picture apart on the puzzle lines. Let the children put the puzzle together. Then give each child an envelope to carry the puzzle pieces home and encourage them to share the puzzles with their friends.

THINGS YOU'LL NEED:

❑ Copies of the puzzle page for each child
❑ Construction paper or lightweight cardboard
❑ Scissors
❑ Crayons
❑ Glue
❑ Business-size envelopes
❑ Clear, self-adhesive paper

Yes, Jesus loves you.
Yes, Jesus loves you.
Yes, Jesus loves you.
The Bible tells me so.

8 MY PRAYER BASKET

THINGS YOU'LL NEED:

- ❏ Copies of the friend figures for each child
- ❏ Paper plates
- ❏ Scissors
- ❏ Hole punch
- ❏ Markers and crayons
- ❏ Yarn
- ❏ Masking tape
- ❏ Stickers, stars, glitter, and glue, etc.

In advance: Cut enough paper plates in half so that each child will have a whole plate and a half. Punch holes as shown in the illustration.

Wrap masking tape around the ends of yarn pieces which children will use to "weave" through the holes in the paper plates. You will need to know both ends of yarn when weaving is finished. Then help them tie a circle of yarn through the hole at the top of the plates so the baskets can be hung.

With colored markers print the words, "My Prayer Basket," on each half plate. Let the children decorate their plates with stickers, stars, glitter, crayons, or markers.

Give each child a copy of the friend figures. Let the children color the figures and cut them out. Help the children print the name of a friend on each picture. Place each child's figures in the basket. Tell the children to use the basket at home by taking the figures out of the basket and praying for the friends whose names are printed on them.

9 SHARING SACK

THINGS YOU'LL NEED:

- ❑ Copies of the four message tags for each child
- ❑ Fabric squares 8" x 10"
- ❑ Yarn
- ❑ Scissors
- ❑ Crayons
- ❑ Wrapped candies (optional)

Give each child a copy of the message tags to color and cut out. Also give each child a square of fabric, a length of yarn, and several wrapped candies (optional). Have the children place the message tags and candy in the middle of the fabric. Help the children gather the ends of the fabric together to make a small bag. Tie the bag with the length of yarn. Encourage children to share the messages and candy with friends of all ages.

I like You!

You're Nice!

I Love You!

I'm Glad You're my Friend!

SCROLL PLACE MAT

10

A.

I Praise
God
for His Word.

B.

I Praise
God
for His Word

THINGS YOU'LL NEED:

- ❏ One copy of the half-scroll pattern
- ❏ Pencil
- ❏ 12" x 18" construction paper sheets
- ❏ Markers and crayons
- ❏ Clear, self-adhesive paper (sold in rolls)
- ❏ Scissors
- ❏ Glue, glitter, stickers (optional)

In advance: Make a construction paper scroll place mat for each child by following these instructions. First, lay the half-scroll pattern on one end of a sheet of 12" x 18" construction paper, trace around the top, side, and bottom. Then lay pattern on the other end of the paper and trace; with pencil lines connect the two pattern ends if needed and cut out if you wish. Write the words, "I Praise God for His Word," on each scroll. Give each child a scroll place mat to decorate with crayons and markers. Some children may want to add stickers, glue, and glitter if available. Write each child's name on the back side of the scroll. To make place mats durable, seal the scrolls in self-adhesive plastic. Cut around the scrolls again, leaving at least a half-inch border of plastic all the way around.

11 PENNY IN THE CUP

THINGS YOU'LL NEED:

- ❑ Styrofoam cups
- ❑ Paper fasteners
- ❑ Heavy-duty thread
- ❑ Metal washers (from hardware store)
- ❑ Stickers
- ❑ Markers
- ❑ Glue

In advance: Prepare a cup for each child by inserting a paper fastener in the base of the cup and attaching a length of thread (about 16") to the section of the paper fastener outside the cup.

To make the game: Give each child a cup and a washer. The children will enjoy decorating their cups using stickers and markers. Glue may be needed with stickers. Then help each child attach the thread hanging down from the bottom of the cup to the washer.

Now try to flip the coin into the cup. Children will enjoy the challenge.

PRAYER POSTER

Give each child a copy of the paper doll figures. Help each child write his or her name on the blank under the first figure, and the name of a friend the child would like to pray for under the second figure. Then encourage the children to color and "dress" the figures to look like themselves and their friends, gluing on scraps of fabric, braid, and lace for clothes. When children are finished, punch two holes at the top and make a yarn hanger.

THINGS YOU'LL NEED:

☐ Copies of the paper doll patterns for each child
☐ Scraps of fabric, braid, lace
☐ Markers, crayons
☐ Glue
☐ Scissors
☐ Hole punch
☐ Yarn

We Pray for Each Other

Prays For

SPECIAL PERSON BOOKMARK

Give each child a figure. Ask each child to think of a special person they'd like to give their bookmarks to. Write that person's name on the bookmark. Then encourage children to decorate their bookmarks with markers, crayons, and star stickers. When the children are through, punch a hole in the top of each figure and thread yarn through to make a bookmark. Children might wish to make more than one bookmark.

Tell the children to ask their parents to help them give or mail the bookmarks to the special person.

THINGS YOU'LL NEED:

- ❑ Copies of special person pattern for each child
- ❑ Star stickers
- ❑ Markers, crayons
- ❑ Hole punch
- ❑ Yarn

14 CHRISTMAS GIFT NAPKIN RINGS

THINGS YOU'LL NEED:

- ❑ Empty toilet paper or paper towel tubes
- ❑ Copies of rectangle patterns for each child
- ❑ Glue
- ❑ Scissors
- ❑ Paper napkins
- ❑ Wrapping paper (optional)

Give each child a copy of the rectangle patterns to color and cut out and three 1 1/2" rings of paper towel or toilet paper tube. Cover the back of each decorated pattern with glue, and wrap it smoothly around one of the rings. Tuck the edges inside the ring and press firmly. Repeat for each napkin ring desired. (Have extra toilet paper rolls and pattern copies in case some children wish to make more than three napkin rings.) Roll up a paper napkin and slip the napkin ring over it to show how it will work.

Option: You may wish to use 3" x 6" pieces of wrapping paper instead of the rectangle patterns for making the napkin rings.

BABY IN THE MANGER

THINGS YOU'LL NEED:

- ❑ Copies of Manger pattern for each child
- ❑ Brown construction paper (optional)
- ❑ Scissors
- ❑ Tape or glue
- ❑ White facial tissue
- ❑ Copies of baby Jesus

In advance: Depending on the skill of your preschoolers, you may want to cut out the copies of baby Jesus for them. Also, if you plan to use the manger outline as a pattern to trace on brown construction paper, to make it sturdier, you need to do this ahead of time as well.

Making the manger—If using copies of the manger pattern, let children color it before cutting. If you are using construction paper patterns, then children need only to cut out the three pieces—one large and two small.

Help children fold the large square on the dotted line; with paper folded, cut the two slits at right angles to the dotted line, then open to a V shape. (See illustration.) Last, insert the two small rectangles into the slits as shown to make the manger stand.

Making baby Jesus—Children can color baby Jesus; then cut out. Give each child a white facial tissue to wrap around baby Jesus as swaddling clothes. Glue or tape in place. Then place baby Jesus in the manger.

Cut Here

16 GOOD NEWS SHEEP

THINGS YOU'LL NEED:

- ❑ Empty toilet paper tube for each child
- ❑ Copies of sheep pattern for each child
- ❑ Cotton balls
- ❑ Glue
- ❑ Tape (optional)
- ❑ Stapler

In advance: Cut out a sheep pattern for each child and cut off 1 1/2" from each toilet paper tube leaving a 3" long tube. (Save the end!) *Note:* The toilet paper tube helps make the sheep sturdier. However, the sheep pattern can be glued into a tubelike shape along the edges and used alone. You will still need one or two cardboard tubes to make the feet (see illustration).

Distribute sheep patterns and toilet paper tubes to children. Help them glue or tape the "body" of the sheep onto the toilet paper tube; fold head down in front, tail in back (see illustration).

To make feet, children will need to cut the end of the toilet paper tube (previously cut off) in half. Help them staple a half ring to the "underside" of the sheep at either end, as shown. As a last step, spread glue all over the body of the sheep; gently tear apart cotton balls and add this to the glue until the body of the sheep is completely covered.

1.

CUT

2.

3.

WIND BANNER

Hand out banner patterns for children to decorate, and then fold along the dotted lines. When this is done, give each child four crepe paper streamers. Show them how to staple the streamers on the inside (see illustration). Now glue the banner pattern closed, sealing the streamers inside.

Next, punch holes on each pattern where indicated. Help children tie a piece of ribbon or yarn (about 10" long) to each hole, then tie all three pieces of ribbon or yarn together with a knot. Finally, tie a longer piece of ribbon or yarn (about 18") to this knot.

Children can hold their banners by the ribbon or yarn and twirl it around.

Option: Fold a piece of construction paper in half lengthwise, decorate with child's name or other saying, then proceed as above. Or experiment with different shapes for the banner pattern (see illustration).

THINGS YOU'LL NEED:

- ❑ Copies of the banner pattern for each child
- ❑ Crayons or markers
- ❑ Scissors
- ❑ Ribbon or yarn
- ❑ Crepe paper streamers (approx. 30")
- ❑ Hole punch
- ❑ Stapler
- ❑ Glue
- ❑ Construction paper (optional)

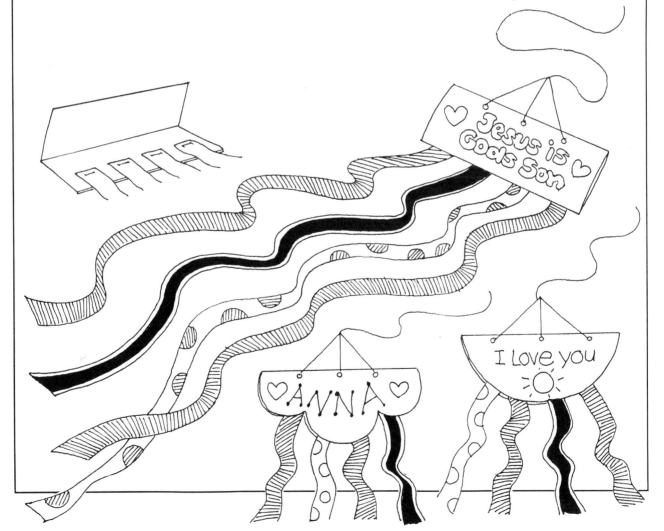

GROWTH CHART

18

Thank You God, for helping me grow every inch of the way.

THINGS YOU'LL NEED:

- ❑ Adding machine tape (or strips of paper 2" to 3" wide) cut in 4' lengths
- ❑ Copies of the head and feet patterns for each child
- ❑ Clear tape
- ❑ Crayons and markers
- ❑ Scissors
- ❑ Yarn (optional)
- ❑ Glue (optional)

In advance: Draw a line down the center of each strip of adding machine tape and cut out the two pattern pieces for each child.

To make the "Growth Chart": Give each child a copy of the head and feet patterns, and a strip of adding machine tape (or equivalent). Show children how to tape the head and feet of the body to the strip. Children may color the facial features and shoes or decorate them with yarn hair and shoelaces.

Attach the "Growth Chart" to a wall. Stand child in front of the chart and mark the child's height. Measure again in a few months and see how the child has grown!

19 JESUS IN THE TEMPLE POP-UP

THINGS YOU'LL NEED:

- ❑ Copies of the these three patterns for each child: the temple; Mary and Joseph; and the view of Jerusalem
- ❑ Sticker of boy Jesus (optional)
- ❑ Glue, scissors, crayons

Give each child a copy of the three patterns to color. (You may wish to cut out the temple and Mary and Joseph patterns in advance to save time.)

To assemble: Help children fold the view of Jerusalem in half, like a booklet. The outside covers will be blank, with the view of Jerusalem inside. Then, glue Mary and Joseph on the outside front cover of the booklet. Next, show the children how to fold the corners of the temple pattern and glue the side flap to make a stand-up building (see illustration).

Now, open the booklet and show children how to position the two bottom flaps of the temple on the diagonal lines drawn on the view of Jerusalem indicating where the temple flaps go; glue in place. (Use only small dabs of glue; be sure no excess glue squeezes out or booklet will glue shut.)

When the children close the cover the temple will fold flat inside. If you open the cover carefully the temple building should stand up.

If a sticker of the boy Jesus is provided, children can place the sticker so it can be seen in the temple when the cover is opened.

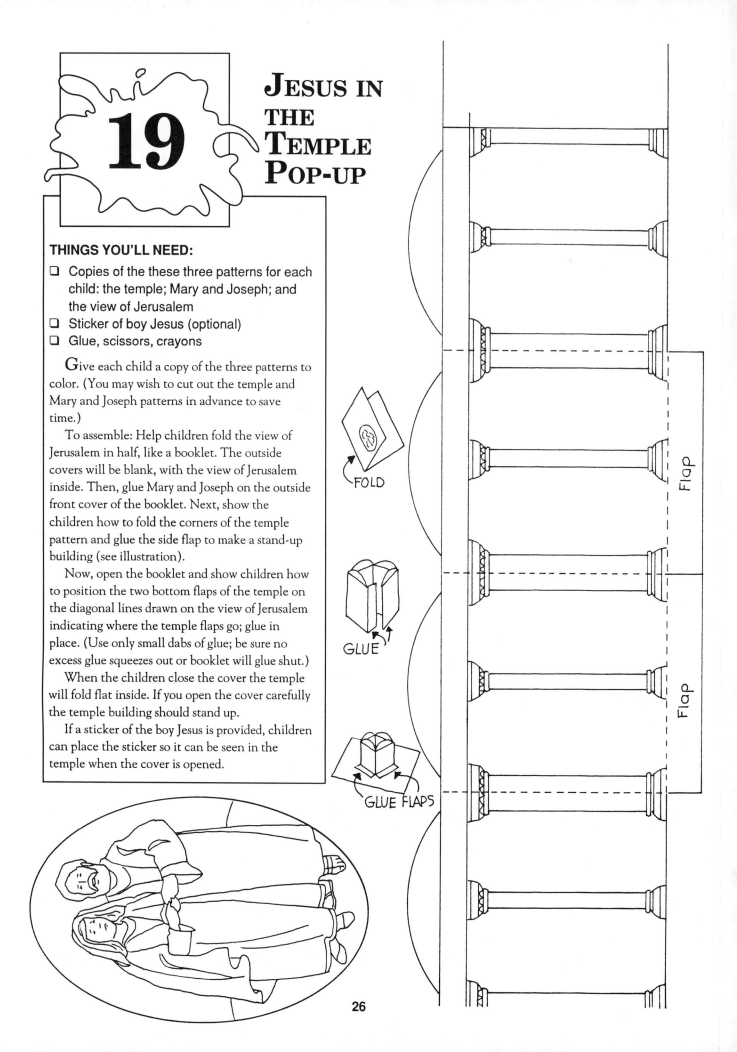

FOLD

GLUE

GLUE FLAPS

Flap

Flap

26

Jesus'
picture
goes
here

Place flap here

Place flap here

20

JESUS IS BAPTIZED STORY AID

THINGS YOU'LL NEED:

- ❑ Copies of the pattern pages, A and B for each child
- ❑ Stickers of a dove (optional)
- ❑ Scissors
- ❑ Tape
- ❑ Crayons

In advance: Cut out the pattern B strip on the solid line. Cut out window and cut away the bottom of pattern A.

Distribute patterns for children to color. Then help them fold pattern A along the dotted lines and tape in back to form a flat sleeve. Pattern B is the piece that slides in the completed project. Now show the children how to insert the sliding piece (B) into the exterior sleeve (A).

If a dove sticker is provided, have the children pull down the sliding piece to the point where the dove should be positioned.

B.

This is
my Son, in whom
I am pleased

Pull Down

A.

Cut
out
window

Fold

Fold

Cut away
triangle shape

21 FISHING POND

THINGS YOU'LL NEED:

- ❑ Copies of these patterns: promise strips (one set per child); "If you follow Me" circle (one per child)
- ❑ One fish pattern to use for tracing
- ❑ Construction paper in several colors
- ❑ 8-oz. paper drinking cups
- ❑ Plastic drinking straws
- ❑ Paper clips
- ❑ Lightweight string
- ❑ Glue sticks, tape, pliers, hole punch, scissors
- ❑ Paper reinforcements (white circles)—optional

In advance: Punch holes in straws; cut paper clips in half and form into hooks; tie string to straws and hooks; using fish pattern, trace and cut out enough fish for five per child from construction paper and punch eyeholes. (Optional: place a paper reinforcement around each eyehole.) Prepare a sample craft to become acquainted with the steps in the assembly process.

To assemble the fish pond: Distribute paper fish to each child. Help them curl fish by running each one over the edge of a table. For more interesting shapes, curl the head and tail in opposite directions.

Next, glue or tape the "If you follow Me" circle to one of the fish before attaching it to the outside of the paper cup. Decorate the cup in other ways. Then glue a promise to each of the four remaining fish. Place the fish heads up in the cup and try catching them with the pole. For harder fishing, place the fish tail up.

I will make you fishers of men	You will have eternal life
You will know the truth	Your sins will be forgiven

MEDICAL KIT

Pass out a paper plate and a copy of the kit and label patterns to each child to color and cut out. Show them how to glue the kit on the paper plate and then fold the plate in half to make a kit.

Next, glue the "Medical Kit" label on the outside of the plate; children's names can be written on the other side. Punch two holes in the top of each half of the plate and help children thread a chenille wire through the holes, and twist to form a handle. Repeat for the other side. When the paper plate is folded, the two handles should match for carrying.

Pass out adhesive bandages to put in the medical kits. (Note: A staple just above the fold on each side of the kit will help keep the "medical supplies" from falling out.)

THINGS YOU'LL NEED:

- ❏ Copies of the patterns on this page for each child
- ❏ Paper plates
- ❏ Chenille wires
- ❏ Hole punch
- ❏ Stapler
- ❏ Adhesive bandages

23 SHEEP LIGHT SWITCH COVER

THINGS YOU'LL NEED:

- ❑ Copies of this page (with holes cut) for each child
- ❑ 3" x 5" piece of lightweight cardboard (with holes cut to match the sheep pattern) for each child
- ❑ Glue
- ❑ Cotton balls
- ❑ Crayons or markers

Pass out copies of the sheep pattern page to each child. Help them glue it to the lightweight cardboard piece so that the light-switch cover will be more durable. The children can glue cotton balls to the shape (be sure not to cover up the spaces for the switch and the screws) and color the sheep's eye, mouth, and feet. Parents can help children cut out the sheep at home.

Send along this sheet so that parents will know how to assemble the switch covers.

Note to Parents

To position the "Sheep Light Switch Cover": Remove the screws from the regular light switch cover; do not remove the cover. Position the "Sheep Light Switch Cover" over the regular one, lining up the holes. Replace the screws to hold the sheep in place.

JESUS' HELPER IDENTIFICATION TAG

24

In advance: Cut ribbon strips to make a loop that will fit around a child's wrist (see pattern for size). Familiarize yourself with the steps in construction by making a sample of the completed "ID Tag."

Assembling the "ID Tag": Give each child an "ID Tag," a ribbon strip, and a piece of clear plastic. Children can color the back side of the "ID Tag" before cutting out the area indicated on half the "ID Tag." Then, assist children in writing their names in the box above the words, "Jesus' Helper."

Next, form loop of ribbon; staple it to the outside edge of the "ID Tag" (be careful that ends do not show through frame when tag is folded. Fold "ID Tag" on middle line so child's name and message shows through the frame. With glue or staples, seal the window portion of the frame. Children can wear the "ID Tags" around their wrists to help them remember to be Jesus' helpers.

THINGS YOU'LL NEED:

- ❏ Copies of "ID Tag" pattern for each child
- ❏ Stapler, glue or tape
- ❏ Ribbon
- ❏ Pencils or pens
- ❏ 1 1/2" x 2 1/2" pieces of clear plastic

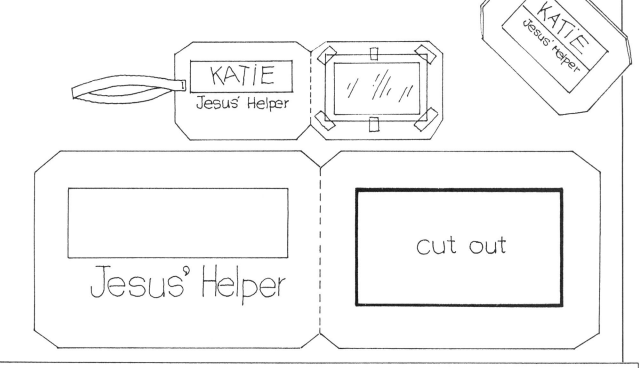

KATIE
Jesus' Helper

KATIE
Jesus' Helper

Jesus' Helper

cut out

ID Tag Wrist Loop

25 TREASURE JAR

THINGS YOU'LL NEED:

- ❑ Clean glass jars
- ❑ Strips of pretty material
- ❑ Yarn, ribbon, lace, or rick-rack
- ❑ Sequins or metallic stickers
- ❑ Scissors
- ❑ White glue
- ❑ Permanent marker

Cut strips of brightly colored material the height and width of the jars you are using. Help children make a thin outline of glue on the material and press it into place on the jars.

Next, show them how to glue strips of ribbon or other trims around the jar. They can add sequins or bright, metallic stickers for decoration.

Write each child's initials on the bottom of the jar with permanent marker. Encourage children to keep small treasures, like pretty rocks, marbles, pins, even pennies, in their jars.

These brightly decorated jars can (1) remind children of the valuable treasure (special perfume) a woman poured on Jesus' feet to show her love, (2) be given as a gift for a special occasion, or (3) be used to keep treasures in.

Prayer Reminder Wind Chime

In advance: Cut about twelve strands of different-colored ribbon for each child. Fold the bunch of ribbons in half and wrap it with a rubber band several times just below the fold, forming a loop (see illustration). Open a paper clip, and slide the bottom curve through the ribbon loop. Straighten the top curve, and poke the wire through the bottom of a Styrofoam cup. Now rebend the top wire, forming a hook for the wind chime.

Give each child three jingle bells to tie to three strands of ribbon. Have children cut out and color the label, "I Will Pray for My Friends," and glue or tape it to the front of their cups. They might like to add stickers, too. When the wind blows through the ribbons and bells of this colorful wind chime, the soft, tinkling sound will remind children to pray for their friends.

THINGS YOU'LL NEED:

- ❑ Copies of the "I Will Pray for My Friends" label for each child
- ❑ Styrofoam cups
- ❑ Spools of curling ribbon
- ❑ Rubber bands
- ❑ Paper clips
- ❑ Small jingle bells
- ❑ Glue or tape

27 GOD'S BEAUTIFUL PLANTS

THINGS YOU'LL NEED:

- ❑ Copies of this picture for each child
- ❑ 1"-square tissue paper pieces in various colors
- ❑ Markers (no crayons, please)
- ❑ Glue
- ❑ Scissors

Pass out copies of the picture for each child to color. (We're using markers only because glue and tissue do not stick to crayon very well.) Show children how to twist the tissue paper pieces slightly in the middle and glue them on the plants in the pictures for leaves, flowers, and fruit.

GOD'S ANIMALS MOBILE

28

THINGS YOU'LL NEED:

- ❑ Copies of the animal face patterns and "God's Animals" message strip for each child
- ❑ Crayons and markers
- ❑ Scissors
- ❑ Yarn or ribbon
- ❑ Hole punch
- ❑ Tape, stapler (optional)

Give a copy of the animal faces and message strip to each child to color. Then, assist children as needed with cutting them out. Hole punch all "X"s as indicated.

Provide brightly colored pieces of yarn or ribbon, and help the children thread the yarn through the punched holes in the top of the animal face circles and tie. Then, help them thread the other end of the yarn through the holes on the bottom of the message strip. Tape or staple if necessary.

Bend the strip of paper into a circle and tape the ends together (see illustration). Attach three lengths of yarn to the top of the circle, tying them together to hang the mobile.

29 FINGER PUPPET FRIENDS

THINGS YOU'LL NEED:

- ❏ Copies of the finger puppets for each child
- ❏ Two 1" x 2" construction paper strips per child
- ❏ Scissors
- ❏ Crayons or markers
- ❏ Tape

Pass out finger puppet pages for children to color. Then help them cut out puppets. Pass out the construction paper strips and help children tape them into tube shapes. Show them how to attach tubes to puppets and then put the puppets on their index fingers. The children might enjoy naming the puppets, or making up stories to tell using the puppets.

PLANT REMINDER

Distribute a set of faces and three straws to each child. The children can color the faces, then cut them out. Help the children tape the faces to the straws. You might add wiggle eyes to the faces and yarn for hair.

THINGS YOU'LL NEED:

❏ Copies of the "Water Me" faces for each child
❏ Plastic drinking straws
❏ Crayons or markers
❏ Scissors
❏ Tape
❏ Wiggle eyes, yarn (optional)

30a CREATION WINDOW

THINGS YOU'LL NEED:

- ❑ Copies of window circle patterns for each child
- ❑ Paper plates
- ❑ Magazine pictures of things God has created
- ❑ Paper fastener
- ❑ Crayons
- ❑ Scissors
- ❑ Glue or tape
- ❑ Stickers

Each child can glue magazine pictures of things God has created in the center of a paper plate. Pictures can overlap, like a collage. Help them decorate then cut out the window circles and attach them to the center of the plates with paper fasteners. Decorate with stickers. Turn the window so it reveals the magazine pictures and celebrate the wonders of God's creation!

JESUS PUZZLE

Give each child a copy of the "Jesus Puzzle" to color. Then help them glue the picture to a piece of lightweight cardboard the same size. After allowing time for the glue to dry, help the children cut the picture apart on the heavy lines. Encourage them to put the puzzle together. Provide envelopes for the children to put their puzzle pieces in to take home.

THINGS YOU'LL NEED:

- ❏ Copies of the "Jesus Puzzle" for each child
- ❏ 8 1/2" x 7" pieces of lightweight cardboard
- ❏ Crayons
- ❏ Glue
- ❏ Scissors
- ❏ Large envelopes

32 MY JESUS BOOK

Give each child a copy of the "My Jesus Book" page. Let the children color the pictures. Help the children fold the page to make a book. Now add these "touch-and-feel" items: aluminum foil for the crown; straw in the manger; scraps of cloth for clothes on the children listening to Jesus; and sand for the "ground" (see illustration).

THINGS YOU'LL NEED:

❑ Copies of the "My Jesus Book" page for each child
❑ Crayons
❑ Glue
❑ Items for "touch-and-feel": aluminum foil, straw, scraps of cloth, sand

Jesus came to tell people that God loves them.

God sent Jesus to us.

The people praised God for Jesus the King.

Jesus Is Our King!

33 EASTER DOORKNOB REMINDER

THINGS YOU'LL NEED:

- ❑ Copies of the doorknob reminder decorations for each child
- ❑ Paper plates
- ❑ Crayons
- ❑ Scissors
- ❑ Glue

In advance: Cut out a 2 1/2" hole, with slit extending down, near the top of each paper plate (one plate for each child) as shown. This will enable the plate to be slipped over a doorknob.

To assemble the doorknob reminder: Give each child a precut paper plate and copies of the decorations to color and cut out. Help the children glue the picture and word shapes on the paper plate beneath the cutout circle. The children might also color the edges of the paper plate. Tell them to hang the paper plates on their doorknobs at home to remind them that Jesus is alive.

Jesus Is Alive

BIBLE STORYBOOK

Let children color the story and title decorations. Give each child a sheet of construction paper. Show children how to fold the page and construction paper in half together to make a booklet. Help the children cut out the title decoration and glue it to the cover of the booklet. Inside, they can glue the Bible story.

If you wish, add blank pages to the booklets so children can dictate other Bible stories to their families and draw pictures to illustrate the stories.

THINGS YOU'LL NEED:

- ❑ Copies of the Bible story and title decoration for each child
- ❑ Blank paper (optional)
- ❑ Construction paper
- ❑ Crayons
- ❑ Scissors
- ❑ Hole punch, bright-colored yarn
- ❑ Stapler (optional)

Jesus Shows Two Friends He Is Alive

One day after Jesus came alive again, two of His friends were walking to a town named Emmaus.

Jesus' friends were talking to each other about Jesus dying. While they were talking, Jesus came along and began walking with them.

But Jesus' friends didn't know it was Jesus. Jesus said to them, "What are you talking about to each other?"

The men stopped walking and looked at Jesus. One of them said, "Don't you know what happened?"

Jesus asked, "What has happened?"

The men said, "Our Friend, Jesus, was put to death and buried in a tomb. Then, some women went to His tomb and His body was gone. They said an angel told them He is alive. But we have not seen Him."

Jesus said, "Listen to what the Scriptures say." And Jesus explained to them what the Scriptures said about Him. He told them that it was true that He was alive.

GOOD NEWS NECKLACE

Give each child a precut cardboard circle and a copy of the two circle decorations to color and cut out. Help them glue their two circles to the front and back of the cardboard circles (see illustration).

Punch a hole in the top of each completed decoration. Thread a 24" length of yarn through the hole. Let the children string cereal O's or colored macaroni on the lengths of yarn. Tie the necklace on the children.

THINGS YOU'LL NEED:

- ☐ Copies of the two circle decorations for each child
- ☐ One 3" lightweight cardboard circle for each child
- ☐ Crayons
- ☐ Scissors
- ☐ Glue
- ☐ Hole punch
- ☐ Yarn
- ☐ Colored macaroni or cereal O's

CUT

MY LITTLE HOUSE

36

THINGS YOU'LL NEED:

- ❑ Copies of the house and people patterns for each child
- ❑ Crayons and markers
- ❑ Scissors
- ❑ Tape

In advance: Assemble one house so that children will see what it looks like when finished.

Distribute house and people patterns for the children to color. Make sure both sides of each house are decorated with colors, then help children with cutting out the pieces.

Show them how to fold the house on dotted lines, cut slits, and assemble. After slits have been fit together, tape the base of the house. Now, they can fit the people inside the house.

CUT

37 FRIENDSHIP TOP

THINGS YOU'LL NEED:

- ❑ Copies of "Friendship Top" pattern for each child
- ❑ One 4" lightweight cardboard circle for each child
- ❑ Short (used) pencils with sharp points
- ❑ Markers and crayons
- ❑ Hole punch

Hand out a cardboard circle and a "Friendship Top" pattern for children to color. When they're done, show them how to glue the two together then punch a hole in the center. Now you're ready to push a small pencil with a sharp point through the center to complete the top.

Encourage children to practice spinning their tops; then encourage them to enjoy the top with friends.

GOD HELPS PEOPLE BANNER

38

In advance: Cut construction paper strips and make a sample banner to use as an example.

Give each child a sheet of construction paper and a word strip. Have them glue on the word strip then give them crayons or markers to draw and color the water and people. (Some children might like to make waves from blue construction paper.) Show them your banner so they can get an idea of where to place the different items.

While the children are working on this, staple three construction paper loops (evenly spaced) across the top of each sheet of construction paper to make a banner. Be sure children print their names on the backs. Insert a straw through the loops at the top of the banner; then insert a length of string through the straw, tie a knot in the ends, and the banner is ready for hanging on a wall or doorknob!

THINGS YOU'LL NEED:

- ❑ Copies of the word strip for each child
- ❑ 9" x 12" construction paper sheets
- ❑ Three strips of construction paper (3/4" wide and 5" long) per banner
- ❑ Plastic straws
- ❑ String (24" length per banner)
- ❑ Stapler
- ❑ Glue sticks
- ❑ Crayons or markers
- ❑ Scissors

39 BEST FAMILY RULES BOOK

THINGS YOU'LL NEED:

- ❑ Copies of tablet title pattern for each child
- ❑ 8 1/2" x 11" pieces of plain paper
- ❑ 8 1/2" x 11" construction paper sheets
- ❑ Crayons
- ❑ Pencils
- ❑ Scissors
- ❑ Stapler

Give each child a tablet title pattern, a piece of folded construction paper, and a few folded 8 1/2" x 11" sheets of paper. After children have decorated the tablet title pattern and written their name on it, help them cut it out and glue to the front of their construction paper "book." Staple the plain sheets inside at the spine to make pages on which the leader will write each child's best family rules. It's important to use the child's own words. When the books are complete, the children may want to "read" their favorite family rules to the group. Affirm their good work!

BIRD MOBILE

40

To prepare birds: Give each child two copies of the bird pattern pages (total of six birds). Glue a sheet of colored construction paper to the back of each pattern page. Turn over and let children color birds. Assist children as needed in cutting out each bird with its construction paper backing. (Add more glue if needed.)

To assemble mobile: Tie four pieces of ribbon or yarn to the top of the hanger (two on each side of the hook), and two pieces of ribbon or yarn to the bottom of the hanger. Space evenly. Cut off one inch from the end of every other ribbon. Staple a bird pattern to the end of each ribbon. Your mobile is now ready to hang in a window!

THINGS YOU'LL NEED FOR EACH MOBILE:

❑ Wire hanger for each child
❑ Six pieces ribbon (or yarn) 12" long
❑ Two copies of the bird pattern for each child
❑ 8 1/2" x 11" construction paper sheets
❑ Stapler
❑ Scissors
❑ Crayons or markers
❑ Glue

41 LANTERN PRAYER REMINDER

THINGS YOU'LL NEED:

- ❑ 8 1/2" x 11" construction paper sheets
- ❑ Ruler
- ❑ Crayons or markers
- ❑ Scissors
- ❑ Tape
- ❑ Hole punch
- ❑ Yarn, ribbon, or string

Before giving each child a sheet of construction paper, lay a ruler along the 11" side and draw a border the width of the ruler; repeat for the other side. Write the words "God Answers Prayer" on the borders as shown in the illustration.

Now fold the sheet in half lengthwise and, beginning at the fold, show children how to cut from the fold up to the border (about every half inch). Unfold the paper; curl it into a cylinder with the folded edge outward and the borders at the top and bottom. Overlap the edges of the cylinder and tape to hold.

Punch two holes in the top border directly across from each other and attach yarn, ribbon, or string with which to hang the lantern.

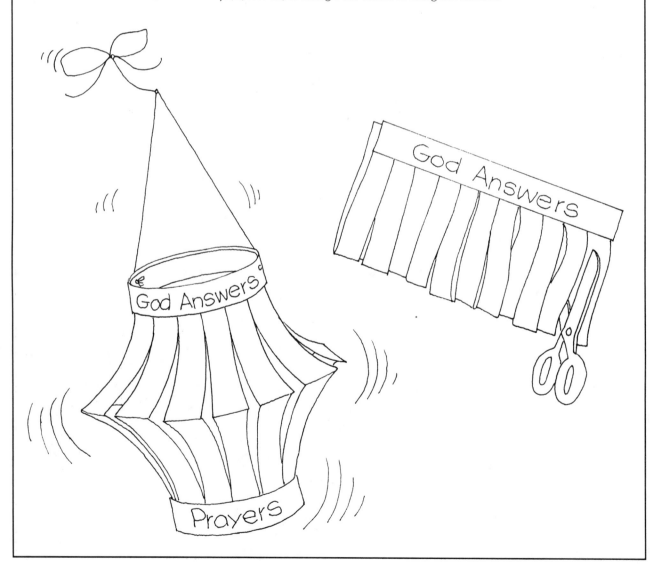

SPUNKY SPIRAL

Show children how to draw a spiral on a paper plate with a big black marker, starting at the outer edge and going around and around to the middle. (See illustration). Assist those who need help with this.

Write a favorite brief Bible verse, or "God Loves You, Daddy," or "I Love You," on the spiral, using the black marker. Again, assist as needed.

Encourage children to color both sides of the paper plate, then cut along the black spiral line. Hold the spiral by the small end and let the large end spiral down. With a hole punch or the tip of a pencil, make a small hole in the small end and tie a string to it.

Children can give their spiral decoration to Dad on Father's Day, or to someone else in the family to use as a special decoration.

THINGS YOU'LL NEED:

- ❏ Paper plates
- ❏ Black markers
- ❏ Crayons
- ❏ Scissors
- ❏ String
- ❏ Hole punch (optional)

43 SAFETY HATS

THINGS YOU'LL NEED:

- ❏ Brown paper lunch bags (some varieties are too small to fit a preschooler's head—be sure to check size)
- ❏ Copies of the "God Keeps Us Safe" pattern for each child
- ❏ Curling ribbon
- ❏ Scissors
- ❏ Glue
- ❏ Tape
- ❏ Crayons and markers

Give each child a lunch-type paper bag. (Be sure to select bags that will fit the heads of your children.) Show children how to turn up the edges of the paper bag two or three times to make a cuff. Give each child a copy of the "God Keeps Us Safe" pattern. Let the children color the words and decorate the paper bag with stickers, crayons, and other art materials. Help the children glue the words to the hat. Help the children make a tassel for the hat by curling several lengths of curling ribbon, tying in the middle, and taping to the top of the hat.

God Keeps us Safe!

OUT OF THE ARK

In advance: Fold the white construction paper sheets to make a "sleeve" for each child (see illustration A). Tape the seam in back (see illustration B). Cut a slit about 1 1/2" wide in the front of the sleeve as shown, about 1 1/2" from the bottom. Then, cut the door in the ark pattern on three sides so it hinges on the bottom.

Give each child a set of patterns (animal parade strip, word box, ark, rainbow, sun and cloud) to color. Then, help children cut out their patterns, assisting as needed. (Or do this step ahead of time.) Now, show children how to glue the ark on the sleeve so that the top of the open door fits slightly below the slit in the sleeve. Help them glue the rainbow over the ark, above that the sun and cloud, and the word box at the top of the sleeve as shown in the illustration.

Next, show them how to insert the sliding strip in the top of the sleeve so the bottom end of it sticks into the cut behind the ark door. Open the door of the ark and slowly pull down the sliding parade (see illustration C). Push the sliding piece back the way it came to close the door of the ark.

Optional: Tape one end of a 15" length of string to the top of the sliding strip; tape the other end of the string to the back side of the sleeve. Pulling on the string will help bring the sliding strip back into the sleeve after being pulled through the door of the ark.

Note: A simplified version of the craft uses no sliding piece; when the ark door is opened, a sticker of Noah and some animals is revealed.

(1) Fold sheet of paper the long way, so the two sides meet in back. Tape shut to form a flat sleeve.

(2) Cut a 1 1/2" slit about 1 1/2" from the bottom of the front of the sleeve as shown.

(3) Cut a 1" x 10" strip of construction paper. Add a crosspiece to the top.

(4) Glue ark over slit on sleeve. Also glue rainbow, cloud and sun, and word box as shown. Insert sliding strip inside sleeve, pull through ark door.

THINGS YOU'LL NEED:

- ❏ 8 1/2" x 11" sheets of white construction paper
- ❏ Copies of the "Out of the Ark" page for each child
- ❏ Tape
- ❏ Glue sticks
- ❏ Scissors
- ❏ Markers or crayons
- ❏ String (optional)
- ❏ Noah or animal sticker (for alternate craft only)

A.

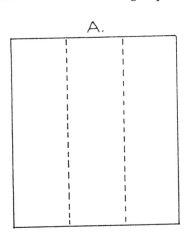

B.

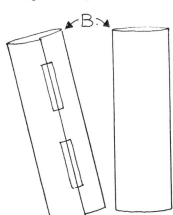

C.

PULL

All
the families
that were
on the ark
returned
safely
to the
land.

SCROLL NECKLACE

Give each child a copy of the scroll pattern, one straw cut in half, a length of string or yarn, and two heart stickers. After they color the scroll, show the children where to place the heart stickers and help them say the completed verse: "LOVE (heart) the Lord your God with all your HEART (heart)." Turn the scrolls facedown and tape the half straws to the ends of the scrolls. Turn the scrolls faceup and roll the scroll from one side only (rather than from both sides) to the middle. It may take some help to roll them tight.

Then punch a hole in the scrolls where indicated and help children thread yarn through to make a necklace. The scroll can be worn around the neck to keep it in a safe place. At home, the scrolls could be hung on the wall as a reminder of the importance of reading God's Word.

THINGS YOU'LL NEED:

- ❑ Copies of the scroll pattern for each child
- ❑ Heart stickers (or red marker)
- ❑ Plastic drinking straws (nonflexible)
- ❑ Colored string or yarn cut in 24" lengths
- ❑ Crayons and markers
- ❑ Hole punch
- ❑ Clear tape
- ❑ Glue
- ❑ Scissors

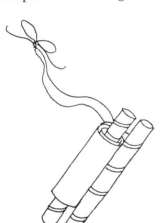

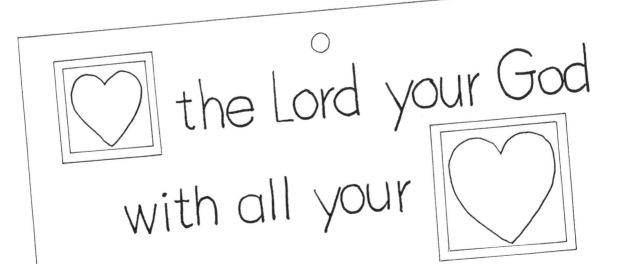

46 SAILOR HATS

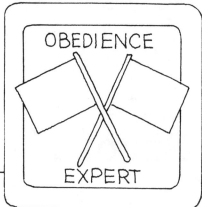

THINGS YOU'LL NEED:

- ☐ Paper (at least 17" x 22")
- ☐ Glue sticks
- ☐ Copies of the five merit badges, one set per child
- ☐ Crayons or markers
- ☐ Five envelopes
- ☐ Yarn and paper punch to add chin straps (optional)

In advance: Make copies of the merit badges and cut out; place these in envelopes to keep the five types separate. Practice folding a sailor hat as a sample.

Help each child fold a sailor hat as shown in the diagrams. Children can color the badges as time allows. Badges can be pasted on the sailor hat as they are awarded, or, if you would rather not stop the flow of the session, have the children place the badges in a fold of the hat as they are given, then paste all five at one time.

Award the merit badges to represent these different accomplishments:

"First Mate"—for following orders during a game.

"Music"—for good singing.

"Bible Verse"—for knowing the Bible verse.

"Bible Story"—for knowing the Bible story.

"Obedience Expert"—for making good choices.

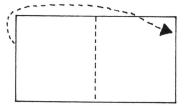

1. Fold large sheet of paper in half.

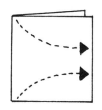

2. Beginning at folded edge, fold corners down to meet in the middle.

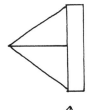

3. Fold up the bottom flap on each side.

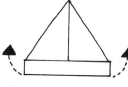

4. Tuck in the surplus flaps.

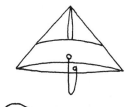

5. Punch holes on either side and add a yarn chin strap.

58

KING SOLOMON PUPPET

In advance: Make and cut out copies of the king face and glue on paper sacks (one for each child). Also cut out black circles and yellow crowns.

Have the children color the facial features of the puppet as follows: beard—brown; lips—red; nose—pink; cheeks—red; eyebrows—black. Next, they can glue on the black circle eyes and the yellow crown. Children can now put their hands inside the sacks to work the puppet.

THINGS YOU'LL NEED:

- ❑ Lunch-size paper sack
- ❑ Copies of king face pattern and black circles for each child
- ❑ Yellow construction paper
- ❑ Glue
- ❑ Colored markers
- ❑ Scissors

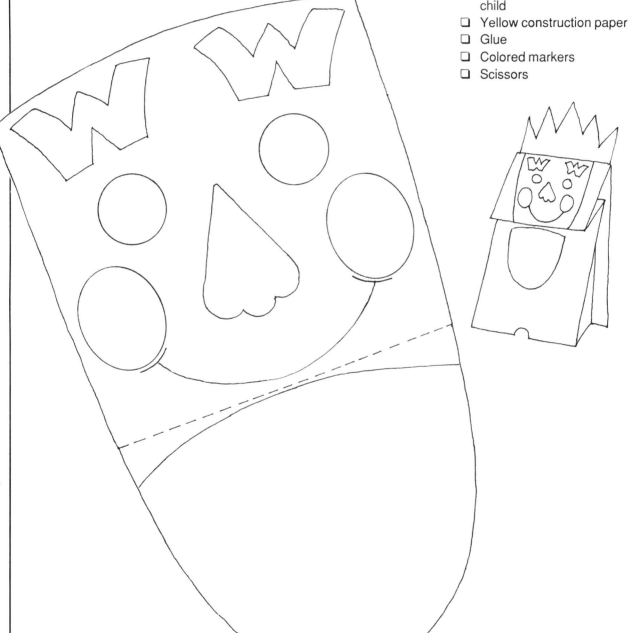

48 SIGN OF GOD'S CARE

THINGS YOU'LL NEED:

- ☐ Cotton balls
- ☐ Black construction paper
- ☐ 3" red construction paper hearts (two per child)
- ☐ White glue
- ☐ Toothpicks
- ☐ White poster paint
- ☐ Black felt pen
- ☐ Safety pins
- ☐ Magnetic tape (optional)

In advance: Cut out sheep bodies from black construction paper (as many as you have red hearts), using the sheep body on this page as a pattern. The ear folds down over the face. Make a sample craft per instructions below.

Have each child put a drop of glue on the back of a black sheep body, gluing it to a heart. Then help them place a drop of glue on one side of a cotton ball and press into position on the sheep body so the head sticks out. Dip a toothpick in white poster paint and place a dot for the eye. With the black felt marker, add little feet, a tail, and a pupil for the eye. Now, pin the completed craft to each child's clothing with a safety pin. Or add a piece of magnetic tape to the back of the heart to attach to the refrigerator door at home.

FOLD-OVER REMINDER

49

GOD LOVE OTHERS

THINGS YOU'LL NEED:

- ❑ Copies of the fold-over strip for each child
- ❑ One heart pattern
- ❑ Red construction paper
- ❑ Dessert-size paper plates
- ❑ Ribbon
- ❑ Glue
- ❑ Scissors
- ❑ Hole punch

In advance: Cut the heart shape out of light poster board and trace it onto red construction paper, one heart for each child.

Let the children begin by cutting out their red hearts. Then distribute the fold-over strips. Teach children how to "read" the words. Then demonstrate how to fold it, beginning with the center fold, as you would fold a fan. Help children glue the tabs marked with an "X" side by side in the center of the red hearts. Then they will glue the hearts onto small paper plates.

Punch a hole in the top of each paper plate, run a ribbon through the hole, and tie it in a bow at the top. Show children how to turn the fold-over pages so they read "LOVE GOD," "LOVE OTHERS."

Children will enjoy hanging this "Fold-over Reminder" in a special place and showing everyone how the message changes when they turn the fold-over section.

50 RHYTHM SHAKER

THINGS YOU'LL NEED:

- ❑ Copies of the Bible verse for each child
- ❑ Dried peas or beans
- ❑ Paper plates
- ❑ Ribbon
- ❑ Sticker stars or crayons
- ❑ 2 1/2" x 4" construction paper rectangles
- ❑ Stapler
- ❑ Tape or glue
- ❑ Scissors

Give each child a paper plate and several lengths of ribbon in different colors. Demonstrate how to fold the plate in half so that it becomes like a pocket. Put a pile of dried beans in the center of the table. Let each child put a handful of beans in the paper plate and fold it shut. Children can hold strands of ribbon in place as you staple the plate together.

Then, give each child a copy of the Bible verse and a construction paper rectangle. Let the children cut out the Bible verse. Help them tape or glue three sides of the construction paper rectangle to the folded paper plate to make a pocket for the Bible verse on the "Rhythm Shaker." Then, show them how to slide the Bible verse into the pocket. The children can decorate the pocket and the shaker with sticker stars or crayons. Tell the children that the verse will help them remember what God wants them to do and they will feel like singing when they do it! Sing several favorite worship songs using the shakers as accompaniment.

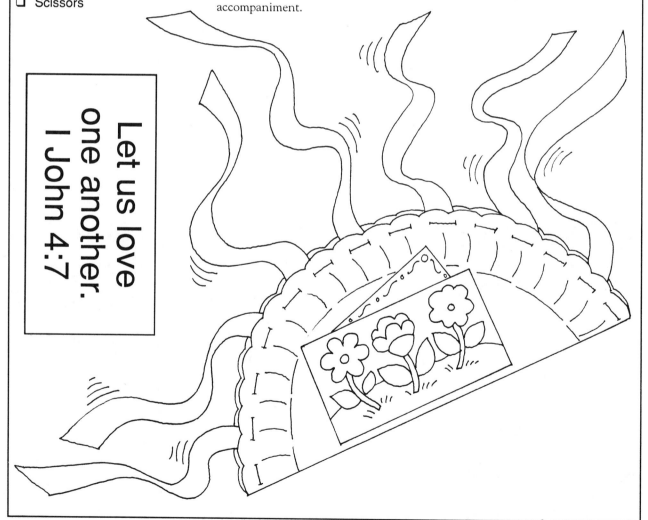

Let us love one another. I John 4:7

OFFERING BANK

51

In advance: Cut a slit in each of the lids large enough for coins to be inserted.

Distribute a margarine container to each child. Pass around markers and have children put their initials on the bottoms of their bowls. Place small piles of macaroni shapes in several places on the table. Demonstrate how to spread a little glue on a lid, then press the macaroni shapes into place in a random pattern. Encourage children not to use too much glue so that their banks can dry quickly.

When the macaroni is in place, have children carry their banks to a large box where you will spray them with gold paint. One side of the box should be cut away to create a space for spray painting (see illustration). Children will be fascinated by the painting process, but have them stand well back to avoid inhaling fumes. Explain that it's very important not to handle the banks until they are completely dry.

Depending on the size of your group, you may wish to put two or three pennies in each bank to reinforce the idea that the banks are for saving money. You might also send the banks home in paper lunch bags, so that the children don't have to handle them until they are completely dry.

Children will enjoy saving coins for their offerings in this special "Offering Bank."

THINGS YOU'LL NEED:

- ❑ Assorted small macaroni shapes
- ❑ Small plastic margarine bowls with lids
- ❑ Gold spray paint
- ❑ Large box for spraying
- ❑ Markers
- ❑ Pennies (optional)
- ❑ Paper lunch bags (optional)

52 SHARE BEAR

In advance: For each child prepare a Styrofoam cup, one large pom-pom, four small pom-poms, two tiny pom-poms, and a pair of wiggly eyes. Write the words, "I WILL SHARE," on each cup. Make a sample "Share Bear."

Demonstrate how to glue the large pom-pom on the top of the upturned cup to make a head. Then glue the four small pom-poms on the front of the cup, forming paws and feet, as shown. Last, glue the tiny pom-poms on the head for ears and add the wiggly eyes.

Tell children to set their bear in a special place where it will remind them to share what they have with others. They can also use the "Share Bear" as a puppet to act out stories about sharing with friends.

THINGS YOU'LL NEED:

- ❑ Styrofoam cups
- ❑ Pom-poms in different sizes
- ❑ Wiggly eyes
- ❑ Glue

BEAR NOSE

I Will Share